Ralph Masiello's DRAGON Drawing Book

Charlesbridge

For my stepsons, Ben and Sam—R. M.

Thanks to all the great educators across the country who have shared my books for so many years, especially Sammie Garnett, Karen Cramer, Marilyn Denison, Ellie Baehr, Michelle Freschi, Dennis Ledibur, Tom Sarver, Richard Beeler, and Rip Cail.

Also in this series:
Ralph Masiello's Bug Drawing Book
Ralph Masiello's Dinosaur Drawing Book
Ralph Masiello's Ocean Drawing Book

Other books illustrated by Ralph Masiello:
The Dinosaur Alphabet Book
The Extinct Alphabet Book
The Flag We Love
The Frog Alphabet Book
The Icky Bug Alphabet Book
The Icky Bug Counting Book
The Skull Alphabet Book
The Yucky Reptile Alphabet Book
Cuenta los insectos

Copyright © 2007 by Ralph Masiello
All rights reserved, including the right of reproduction in whole or in part in any form. Charlesbridge and colophon are registered trademarks of Charlesbridge Publishing, Inc.

Published by Charlesbridge
85 Main Street
Watertown, MA 02472
(617) 926-0329
www.charlesbridge.com

Library of Congress Cataloging-in-Publication Data
Masiello, Ralph.
  Ralph Masiello's dragon drawing book / Ralph Masiello.
    p. cm.
  ISBN 978-1-57091-531-4 (reinforced for library use)
  ISBN 978-1-57091-532-1 (softcover)
1. Dragons in art—Juvenile literature. 2. Drawing—Technique—Juvenile literature. I. Title. II. Title: Dragon drawing book.
NC825.D72M37 2007
743.6—dc22   2006021266

Printed in China
(hc) 10 9 8 7 6 5 4 3 2 1
(sc) 10 9 8 7 6 5 4 3 2 1

Illustrations done in mixed media
Display type and text type set in Near Myth, La Bamba, Goudy, and Rotis Sans Serif
Color separations by Chroma Graphics, Singapore
Printed and bound by Jade Productions
Production supervision by Brian G. Walker
Designed by Susan Mallory Sherman and Martha MacLeod Sikkema

Hello, Fellow Artists!

DRAGON! What image comes to mind when you hear that word? Do you picture a winged, serpentine, fire-breathing beast that wreaks havoc on poor villagers? Well, that's just one small part of the story. There's much, much more to dragon lore.

Dragons have been present throughout human history. Every culture has encountered these mysterious and magical beasts. Some dragons make fiery mayhem, some connect the earth to the heavens, and some help mankind. In this book I'll introduce you to a few of my favorites, from the Australian Aboriginal rainbow serpent to the Chinese imperial dragon.

Follow the steps in red to create the dragons and their surroundings. Then color in your artwork with your favorite art tools. You'll also find some blue challenge steps in boxes throughout the book to help enhance your dragons. With patience, creativity, and possibly a bit of ancient magic, you can bring these miraculous marvels of mythology to life.

Happy drawing,

Ralph

Choose your tools

pastel pencil

crayon

watercolor

fine-tip marker

colored pencil

marker

poster paint

① Aboriginal Rainbow Serpent

② Ouroboros

③ Mushussu

④ Maya Celestial Dragon

⑤ Lambton Wyrm

⑥ Wyvern

⑦ Fafnir

⑧ Cockatrice

⑨ Makara and Naga

⑩ Chinese Imperial Dragon

⑪ Draco Quabbininus Americanus

Author's Note

In researching this book, I became truly amazed at the great diversity of the dragon world, as well as at the unmistakable similarities from beast to beast. Different dragons appear to be combinations of various animals, yet the underlying tie that binds them is the image of the serpent, whether it's a long, winding body, scales, or an actual serpent head. In fact, in some ancient texts the words *dragon* and *serpent* are actually interchangeable.

Did all these creatures rise from one ancient dragon species, or are they different species that coincidentally have serpentine qualities? Or, as some believe, are they just figments of the imagination, stemming from the natural human fear of snakes? Personally, I like to think dragons are real. I believe they may be in hiding, fearful of our modern society—waiting to reveal themselves once again.

— Aboriginal Rainbow Serpent —

Make a colorful and wild Aboriginal design.

Australian Aboriginal people believe in a universe divided into two worlds: the world in which we live and another world from which it sprang, called Dreamtime. The rainbow serpent bridges these two worlds, connecting the physical world to Dreamtime, the earth to the heavens, and the past to the future. The rainbow serpent is perhaps the oldest known continually used religious symbol in human history, predating even the Egyptian pyramids.

Australia

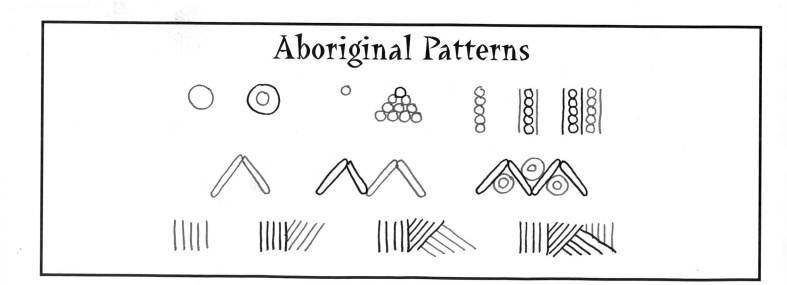

Aboriginal Patterns

marker

Ouroboros

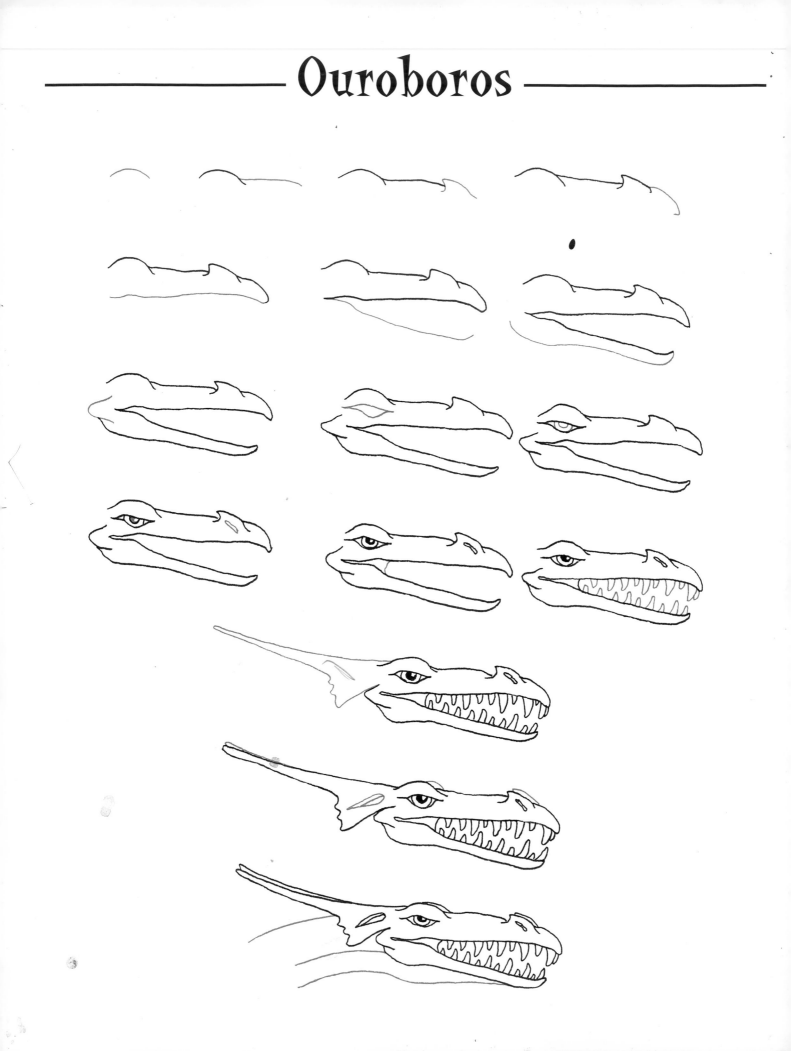

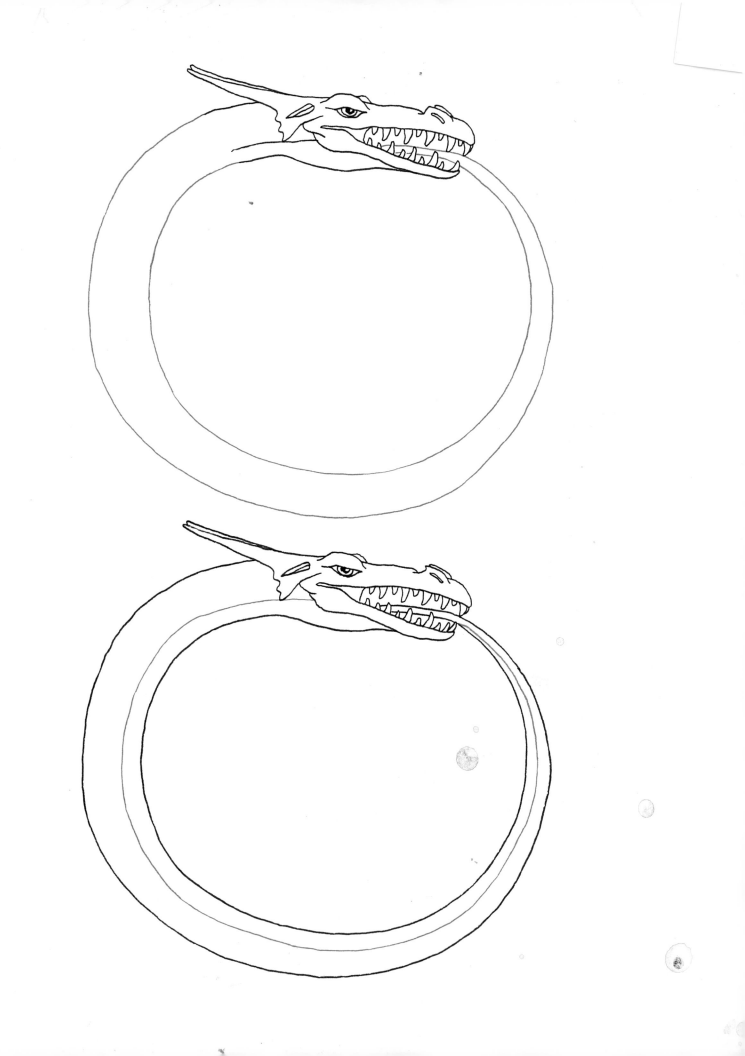

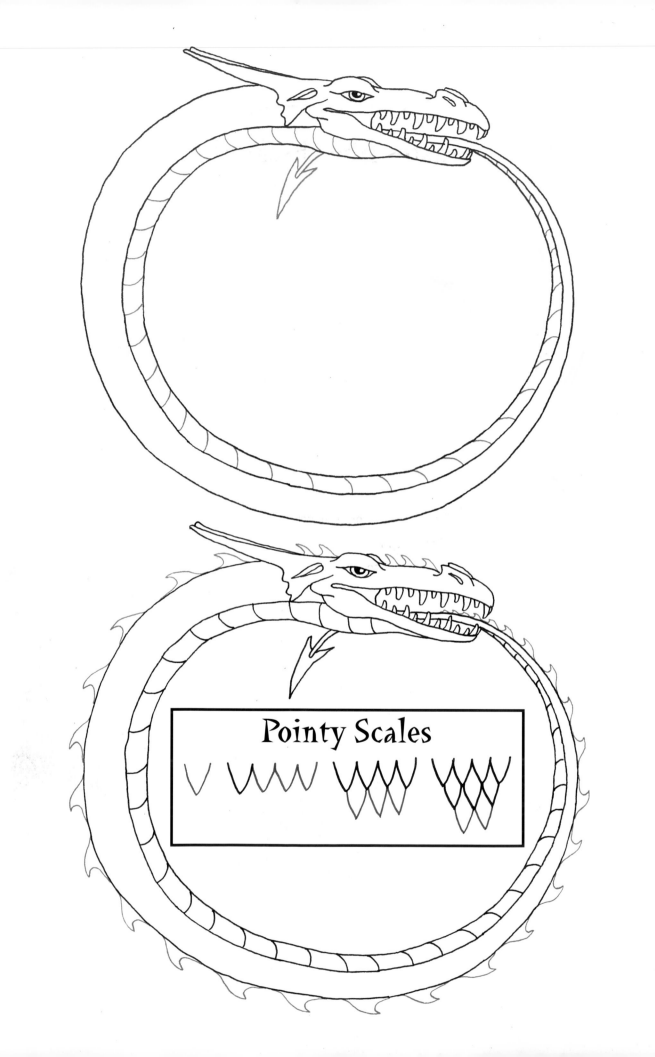

Pointy Scales

Tasty tail treat.
Tastes like chicken!

The ouroboros, or "tail-devourer," is an ancient symbol of eternity. It is a serpent that continually eats its own tail in order to live. The ouroboros is usually portrayed in a circular ring, but it has also been shown in a figure-eight pattern, much like the mathematical symbol for infinity (∞). Some scholars believe that the image of this tail-eating dragon comes from the fiery ring created by the sun during a solar eclipse.

Africa, Europe, India, Asia

colored pencil

Mushussu

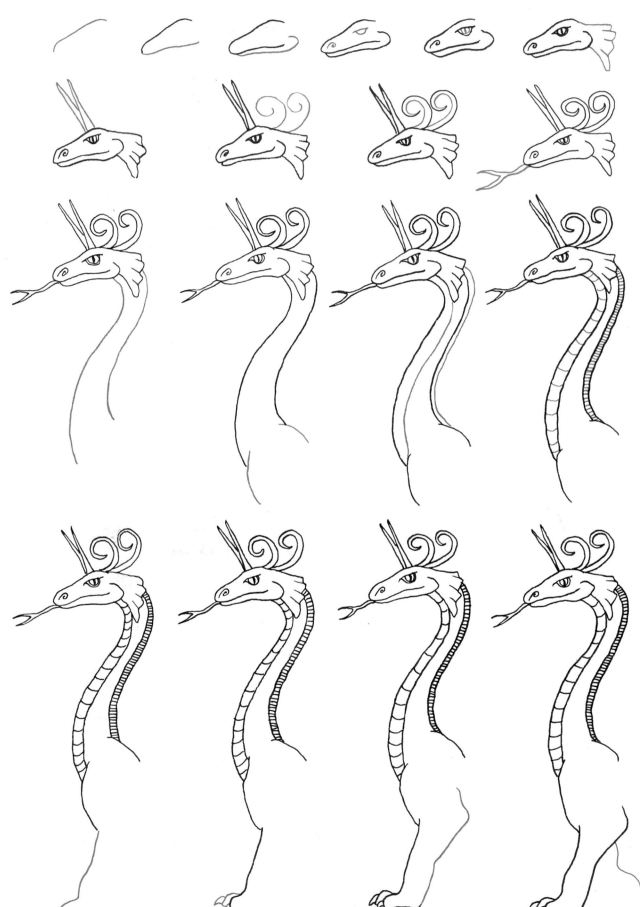

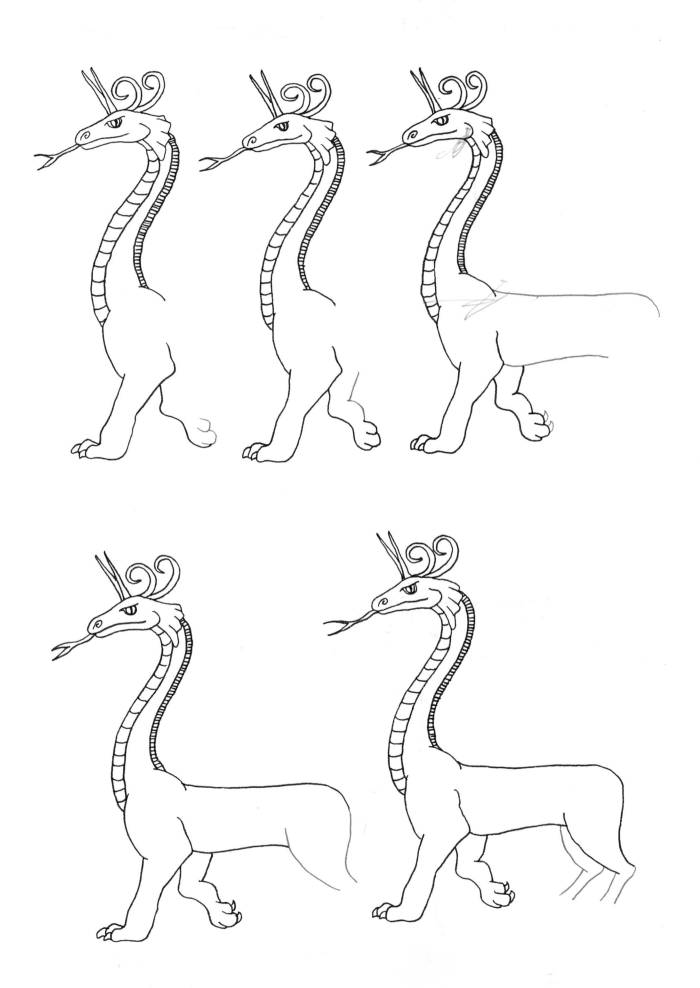

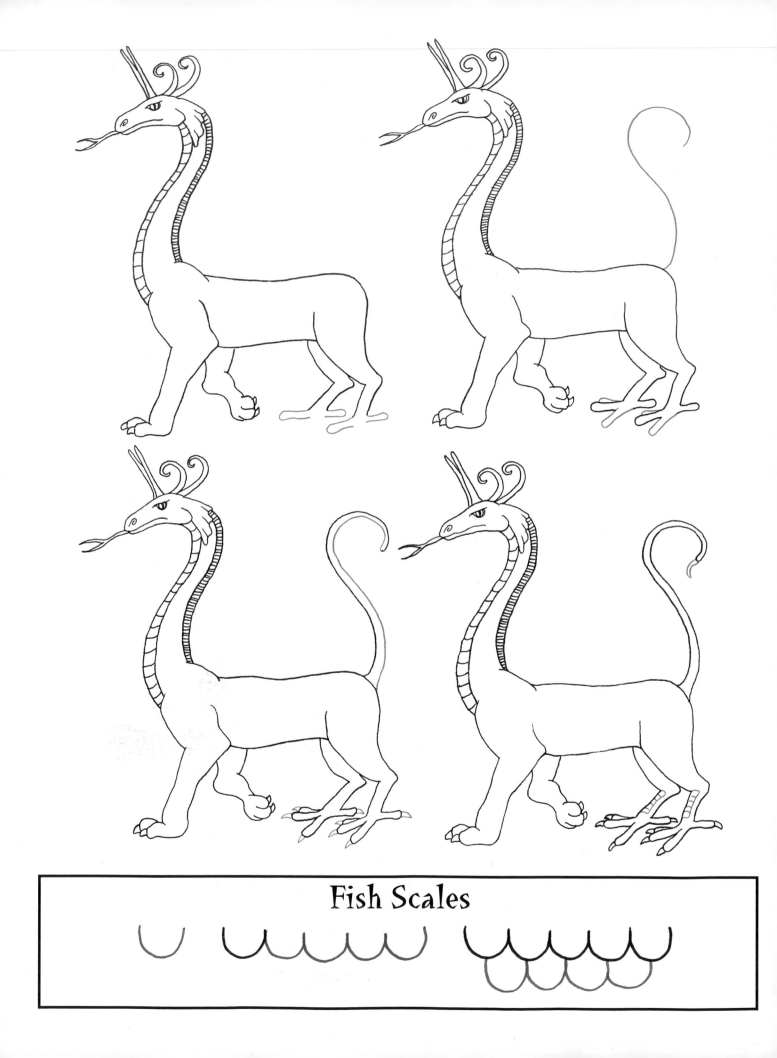

Fish Scales

Dinosaur or dragon? You decide.

crayon

Mushussu, also called Sirrush, is known as the Babylonian dragon of chaos.
In many images and sculptures, it is shown with the front legs of a lion, the back
legs of an eagle, the neck and head of a viper, and a tail ending with a scorpion's
stinger. Some believe that it survived from the age of dinosaurs, living in the
swamps and wetlands surrounding ancient Babylon. In nearly all depictions the
Mushussu dragon looks a lot like a sauropod. The Mushussu is depicted on the
Ishtar Gate of Babylon, which was built in approximately 600 B.C.E.

Middle East

Maya Celestial Dragon

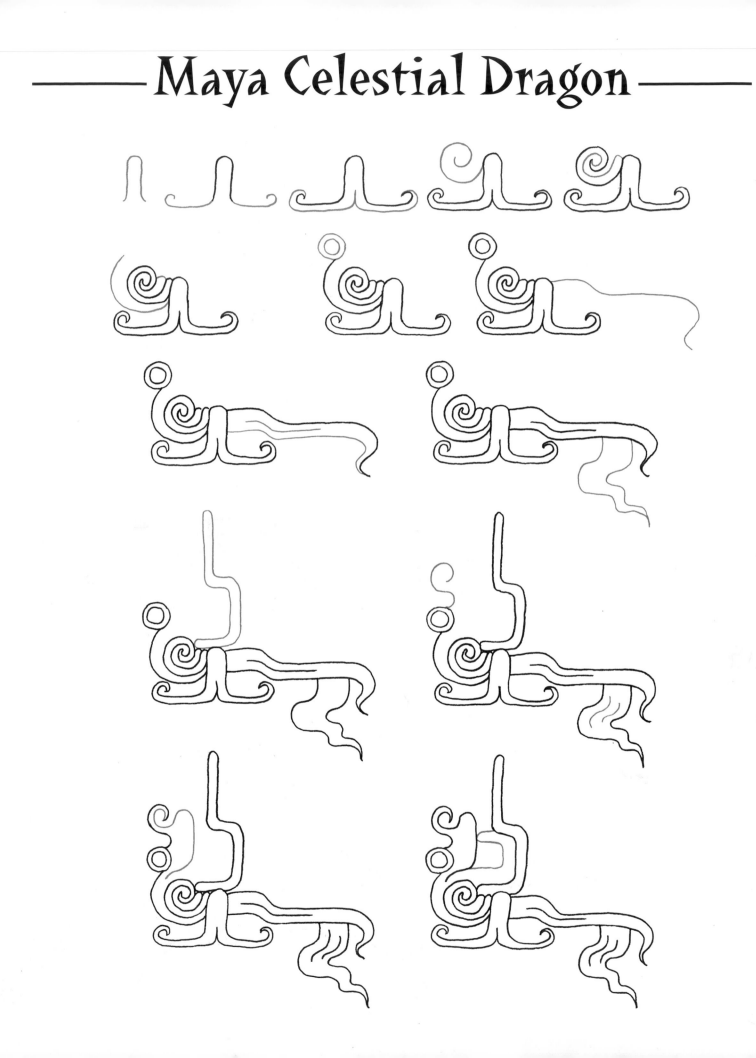

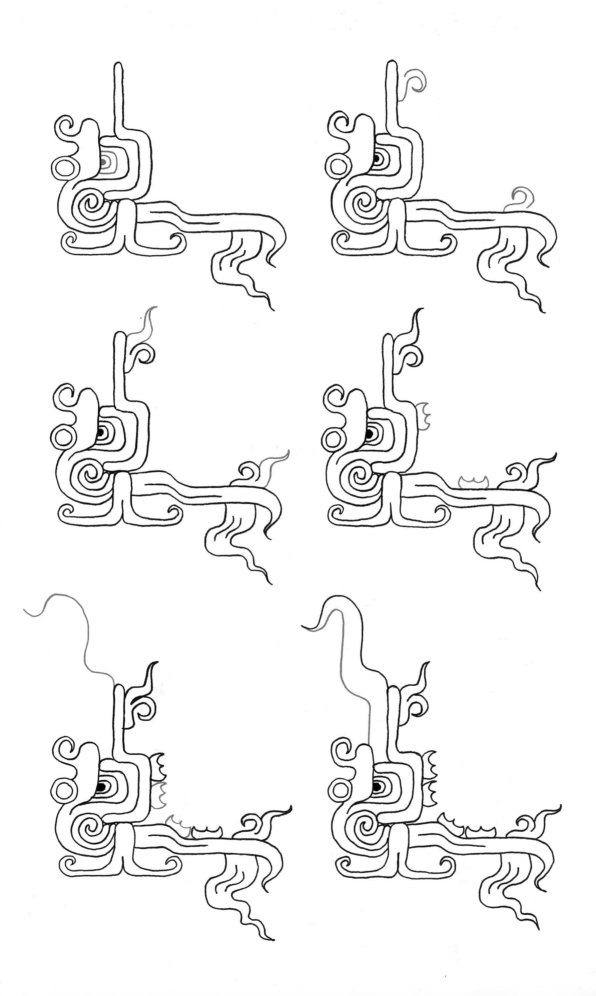

Maya Patterns and Shapes

Nose Plugs

Make patterns and plumes!

The Maya celestial dragon has
the body of a snake, sometimes
covered with the feathers of a bird.
The double-headed serpent may represent
the movement of the sun and planets across
the sky. Its two heads are often adorned
with stylized fangs, plumes, flames,
smoke, clouds, or drops of water.
From the dragon's open mouths
emerge the figures of Maya
gods or ancestors.

Central America, Mexico

marker and colored pencil

Lambton Wyrm

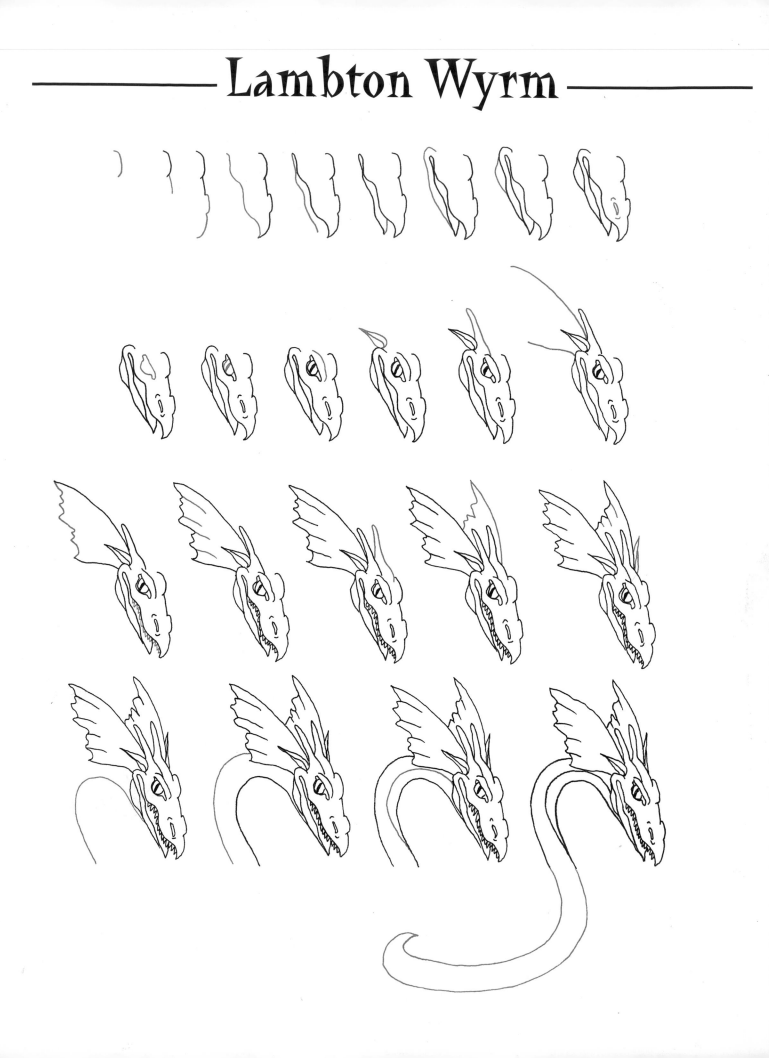

Monument

Bushes

That's a wrap!

As a boy in the Middle Ages, John Lambton went fishing and caught a hideous creature—long, slimy, and black, with a dragon's head. Disgusted, he tossed it down a well. The eel-like creature survived and eventually grew to such an enormous size that it erupted from the well and wrapped itself around a hill. When it got hungry the wyrm would slither through the countryside, devouring cows, chickens, and helpless villagers. This destruction filled the now-grown John with guilt. He consulted a witch, who instructed him to make a suit of armor covered with sharp spikes and blades. Protected by this suit, he slew the dragon.

Great Britain

marker and pastel pencil

Clouds

Wyvern

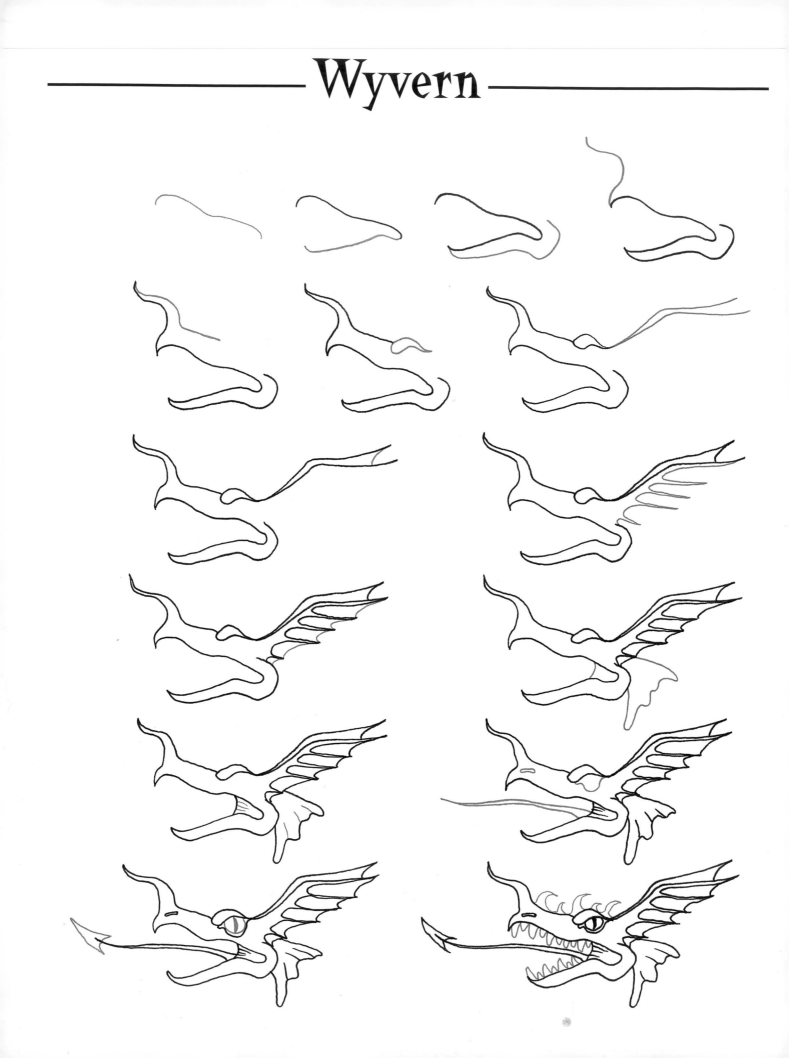

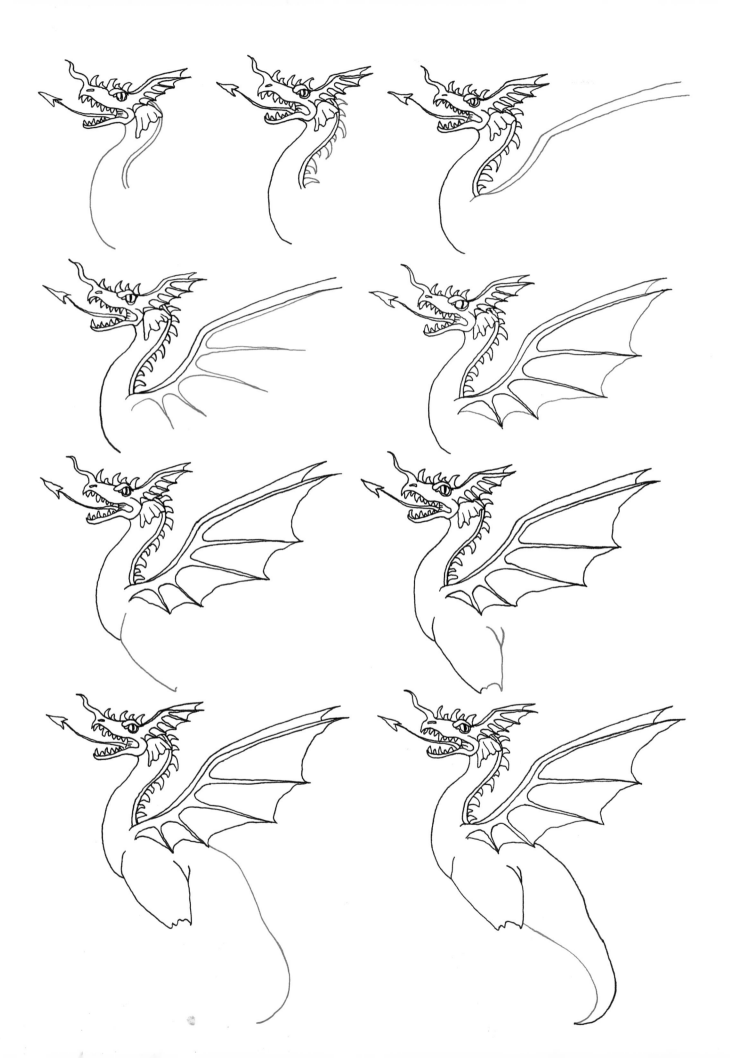

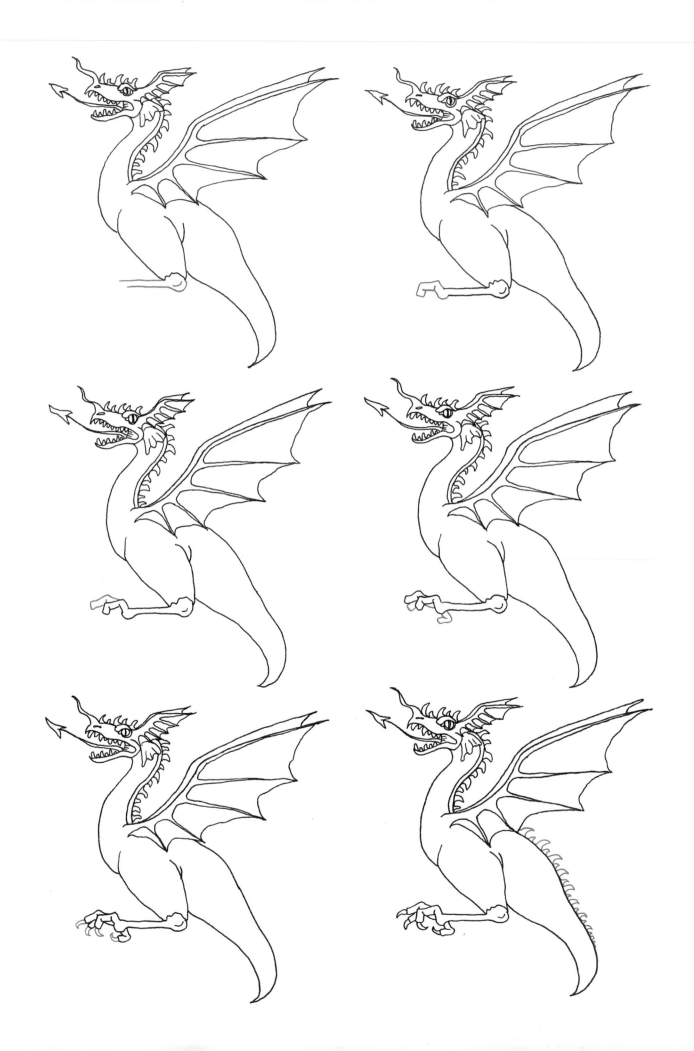

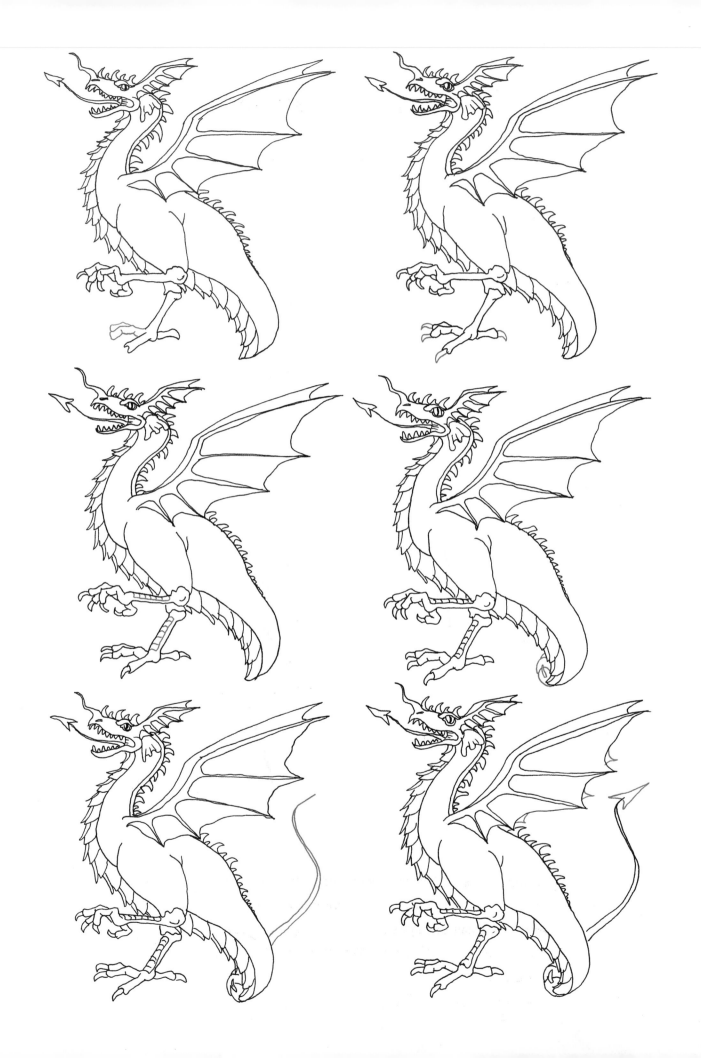

Make a raggedy, scaly creature.

watercolor and marker

Wyverns are mischievous, vicious, and malevolent creatures believed to cause disease and death. A wyvern has a large serpentine body and head, a pair of eagle's legs, feathered or scaled wings, and a barbed tail. Unlike the classic Western dragon, it has only two legs. Some wyverns can breathe fire.

Northern Europe, Greece, and Ethiopia

Fafnir

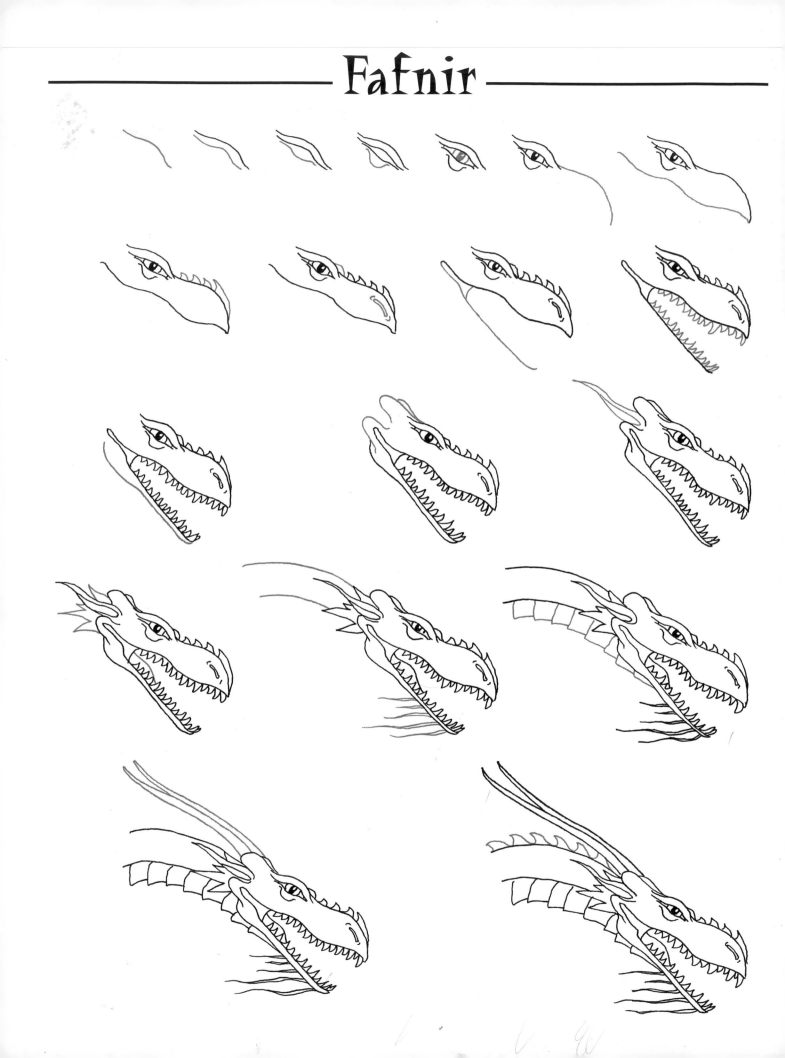

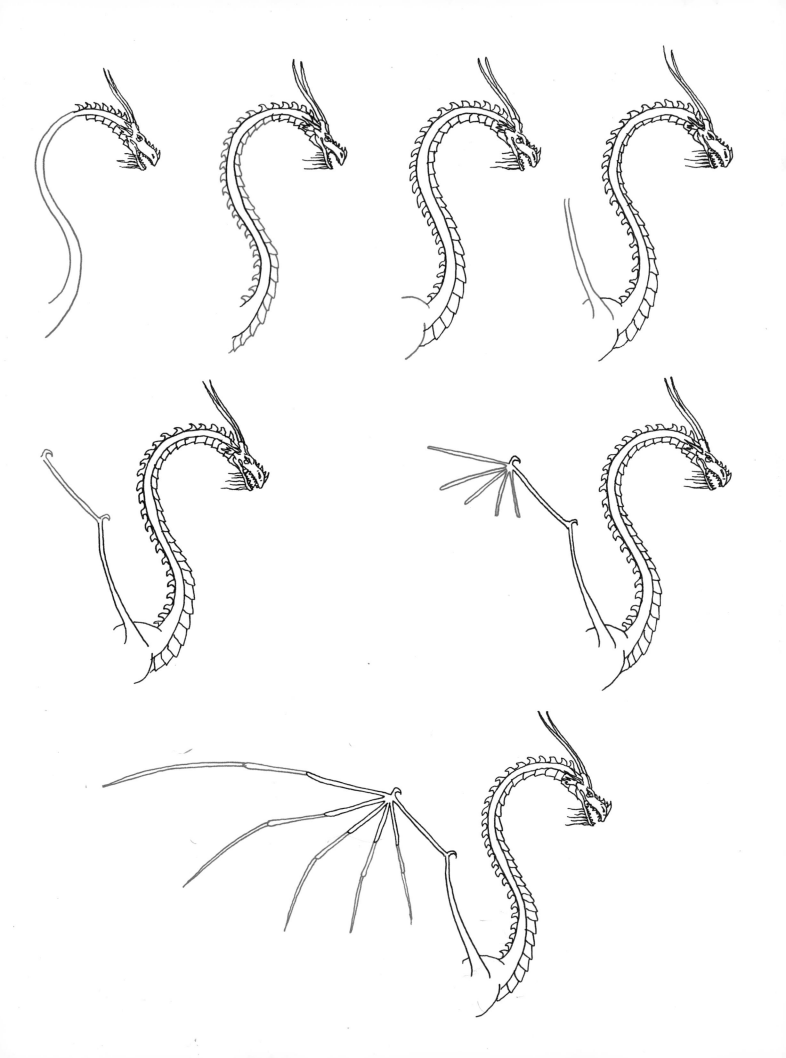

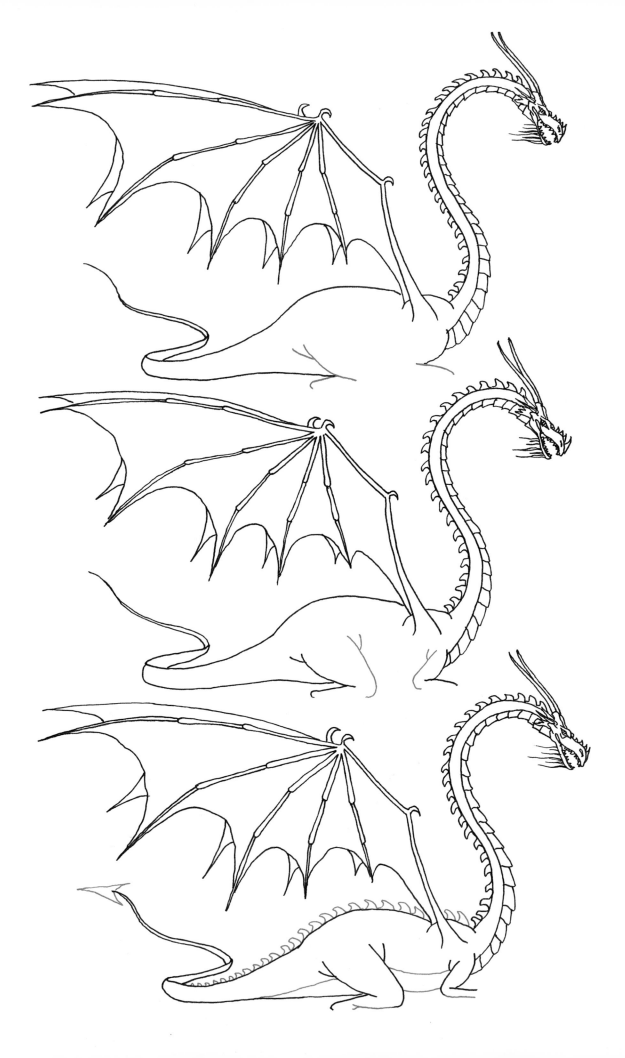

Western dragons have wings, four legs, and the ability to breathe fire or acid. The most famous Western dragon was called Fafnir. Driven by greed, the human Fafnir killed his father and stole his gold, hiding it deep in the mountains and guarding it viciously. As Fafnir turned his back on humanity, his greed consumed him. He slowly turned into a monstrous dragon. A warrior, Siegfried, fought Fafnir and slew him. After the battle, Siegfried licked the dragon's magical blood from his fingers and gained the ability to hear animals and birds speak.

Northern Europe

Feel the heat of greed.

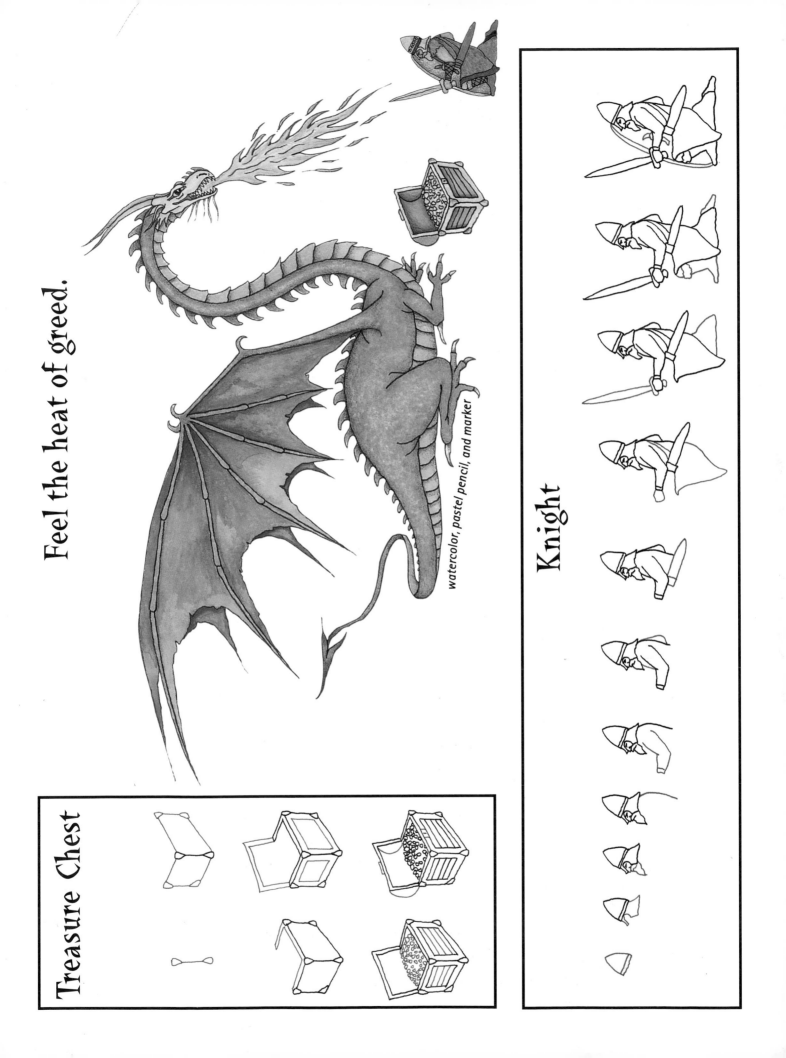

watercolor, pastel pencil, and marker

Treasure Chest

Knight

Cockatrice

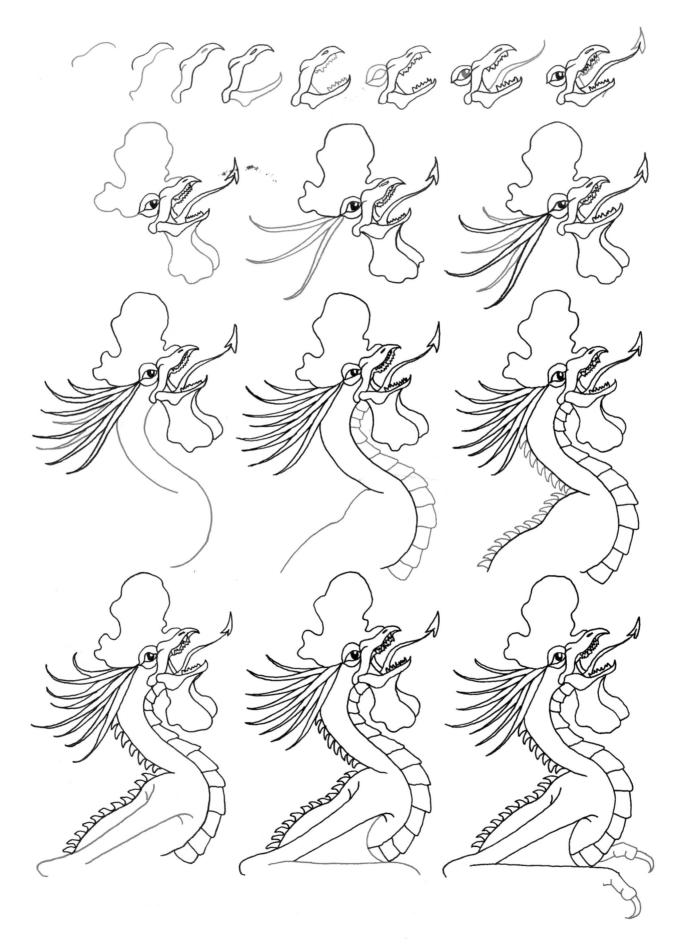

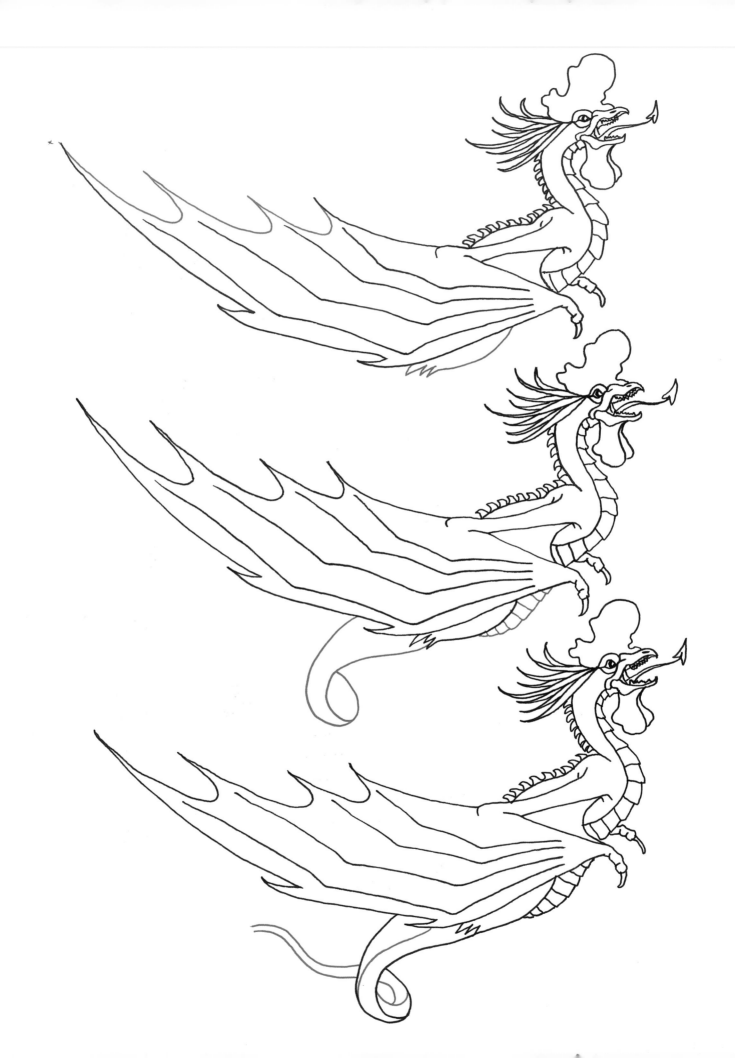

Dragon Tail with Head

Heads or tails?
Add some scales!

marker and colored pencil

The cockatrice is born from an egg laid in a dunghill by a rooster. The egg must then be hatched by a toad. The cockatrice has the head of a cockerel, the tail of a serpent, and the wings of a bird or bat. The look and breath of the cockatrice is deadly, and it can rot the fruit off trees and even pollute the water from which it drinks. It can only be killed by the venom of a weasel, the sound of a rooster crowing, the sight of its own reflection, or the gaze of another cockatrice.

Europe

Makara and Naga

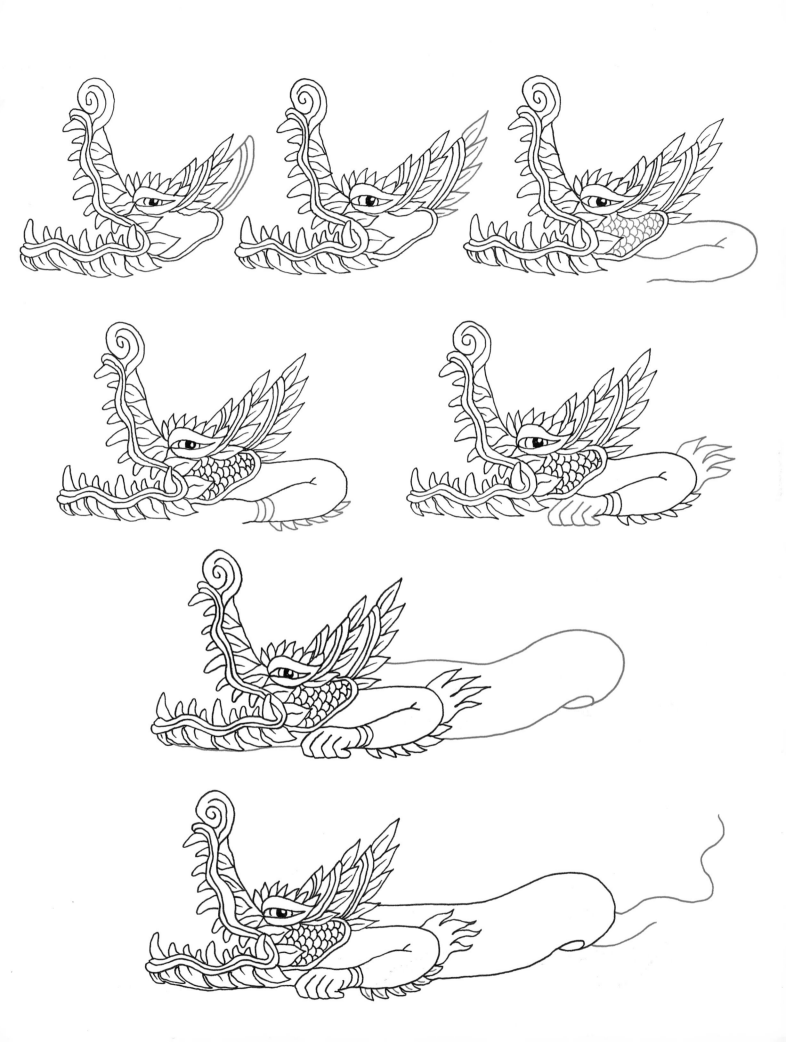

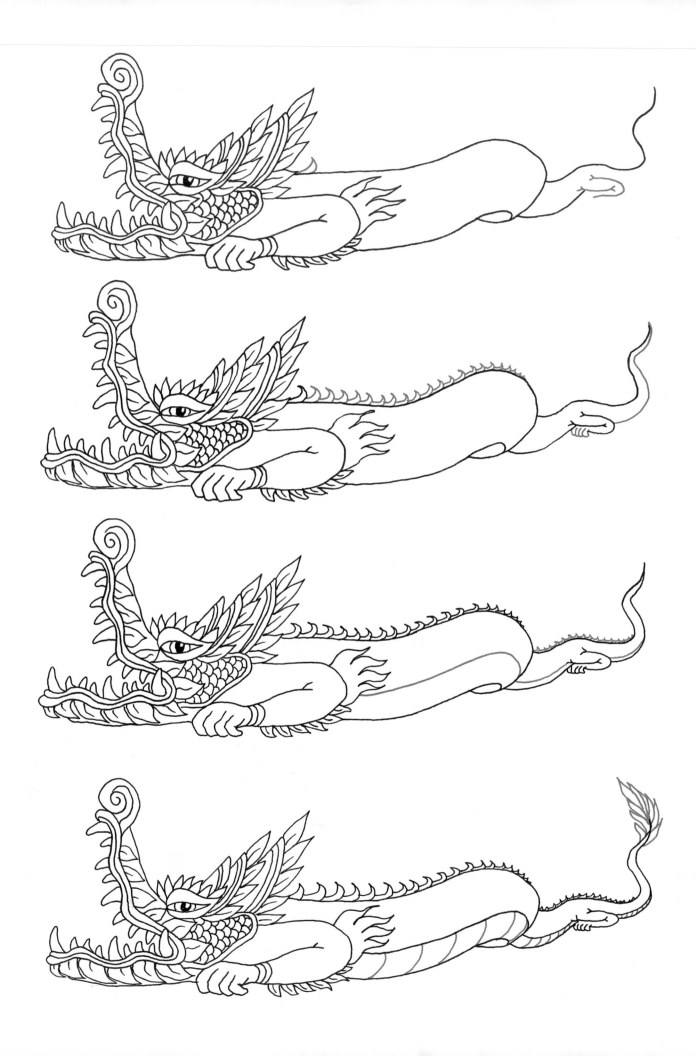

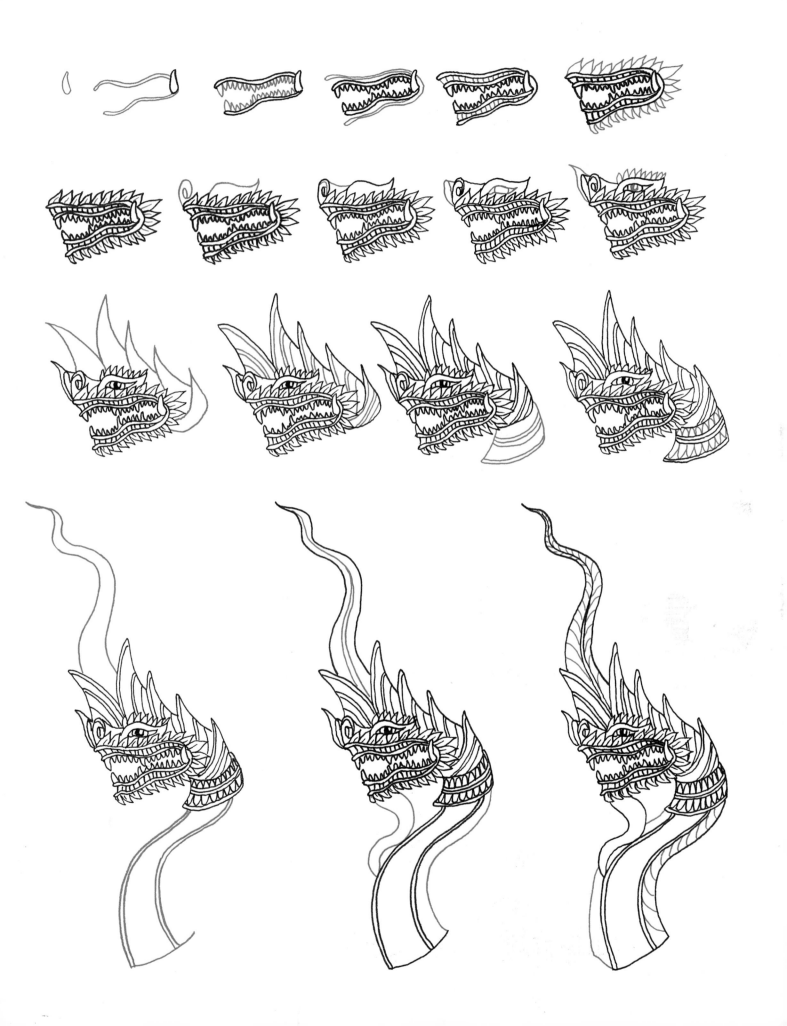

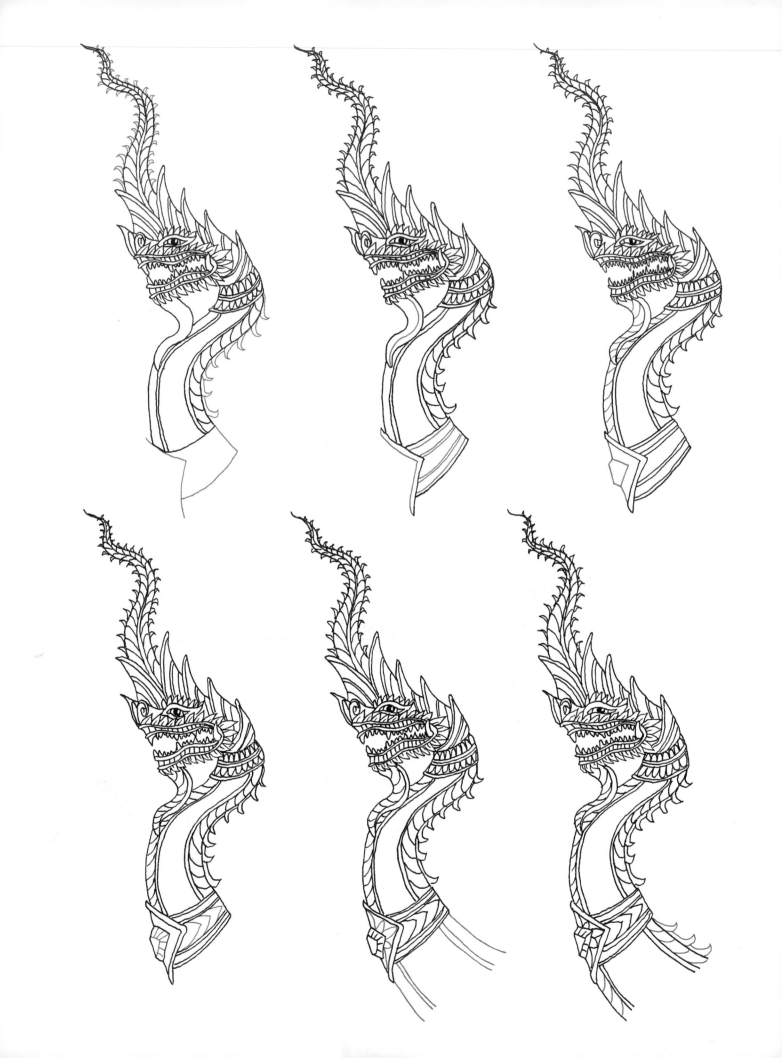

Three heads are better than one!

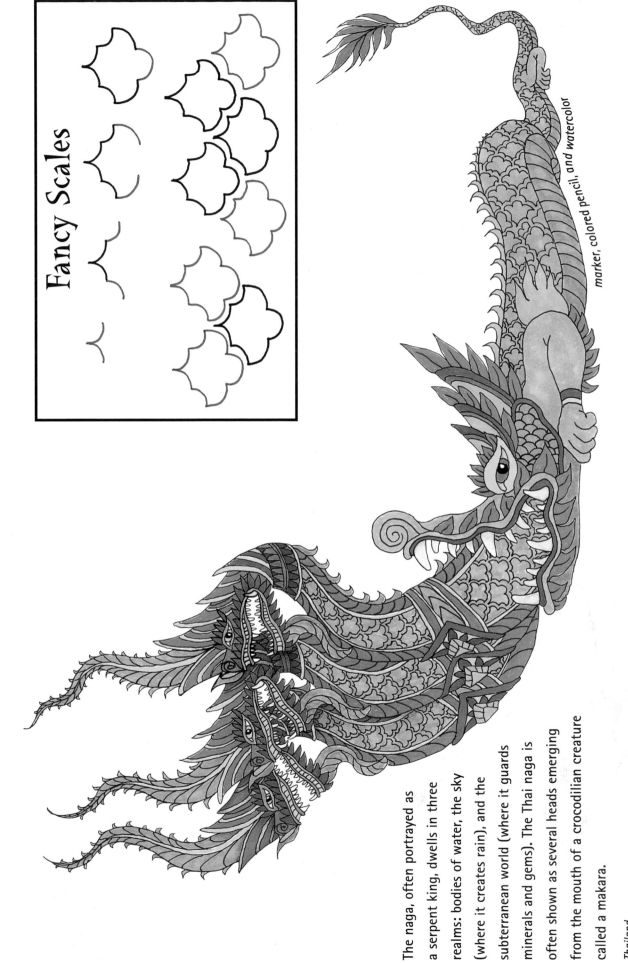

Fancy Scales

The naga, often portrayed as a serpent king, dwells in three realms: bodies of water, the sky (where it creates rain), and the subterranean world (where it guards minerals and gems). The Thai naga is often shown as several heads emerging from the mouth of a crocodilian creature called a makara.

Thailand

marker, colored pencil, and watercolor

Chinese Imperial Dragon

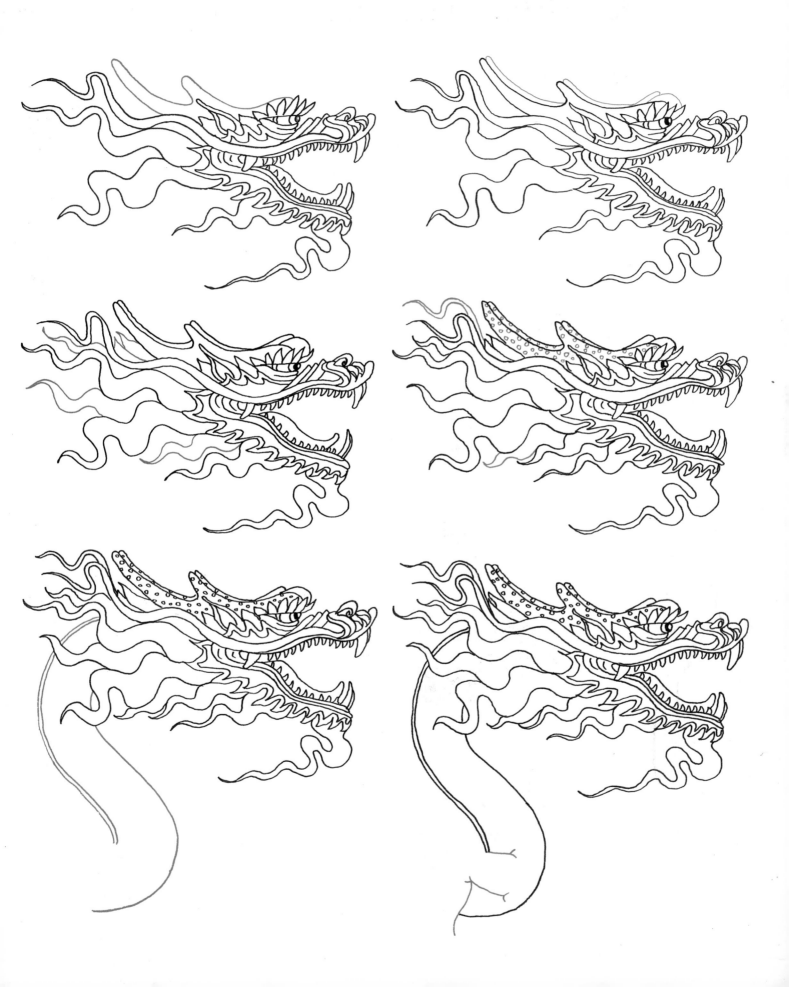

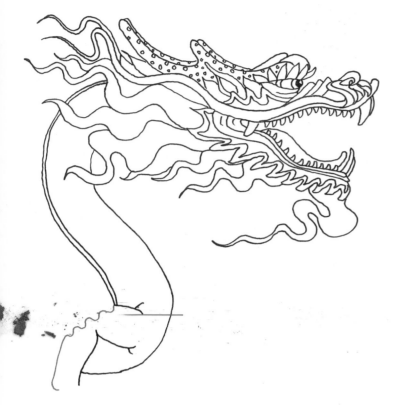

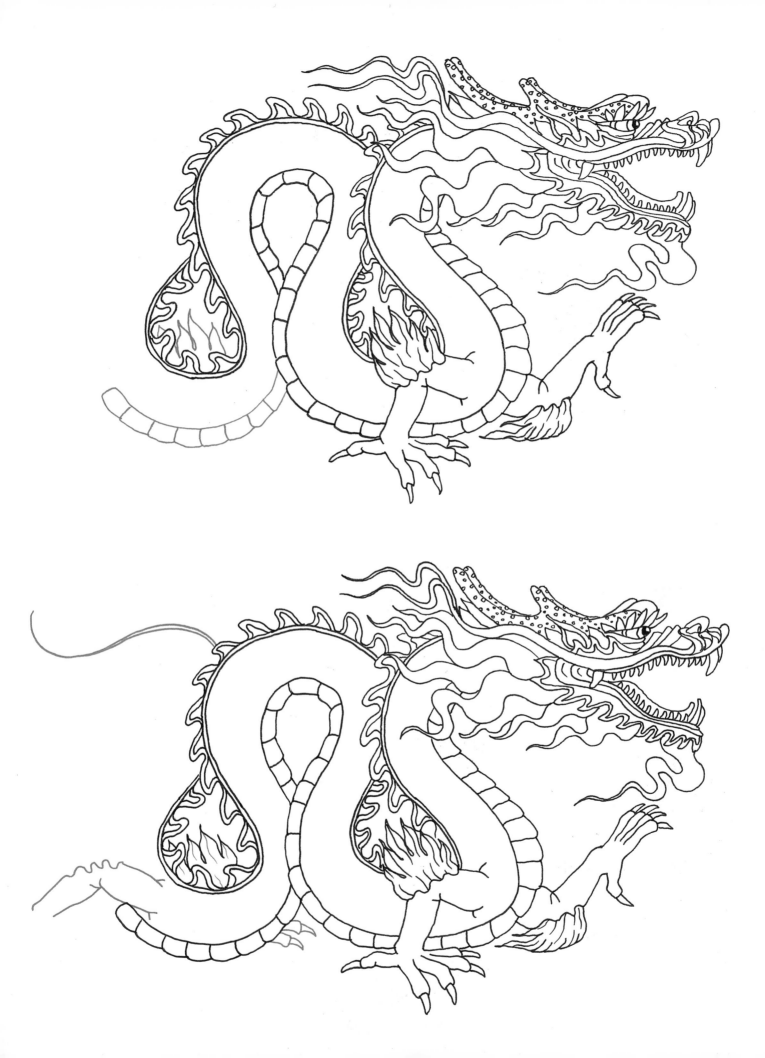

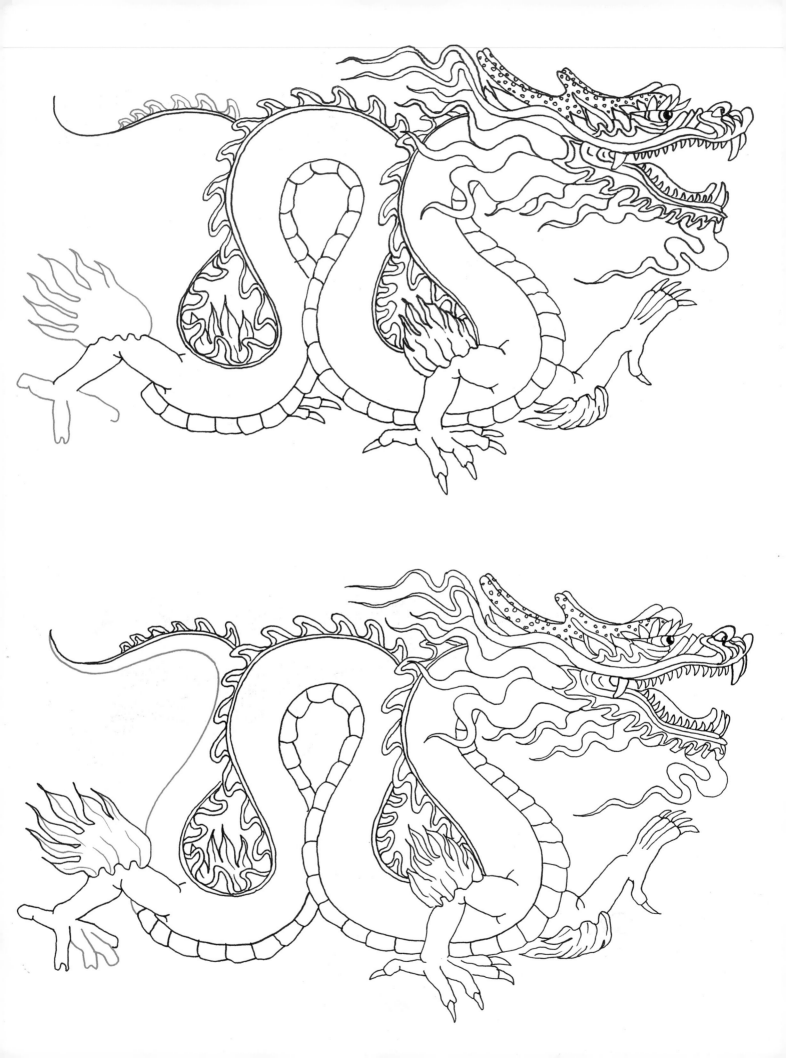

Unlike Western dragons, which are usually malevolent in nature, most Eastern dragons are benevolent, friendly, and wise. Many temples and shrines have been built to honor these creatures, who are associated with life-giving water. The Chinese imperial dragon, called Lung, is a beautiful, colorful combination of many other creatures. It has the head of a camel, the scales of a carp, the horns of a giant stag, the eyes of a rabbit, the ears of a bull, the neck of a snake, the belly of a frog, the paws of a tiger, and the claws of an eagle! The imperial dragon is usually shown chasing or holding a pearl of wisdom.

China

Pearl of Wisdom

Pause to draw some claws.

The number of claws on an Eastern dragon's paws usually indicates what country it is from. Chinese dragons have up to five claws, Korean dragons have four claws, and Japanese dragons have three claws.

marker, crayon, colored pencil, pastel pencil, and watercolor

Clouds and Water

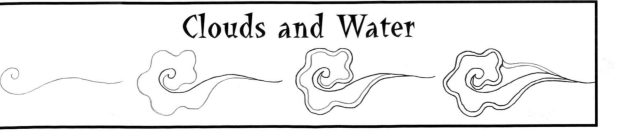

— Draco Quabbininus Americanus —

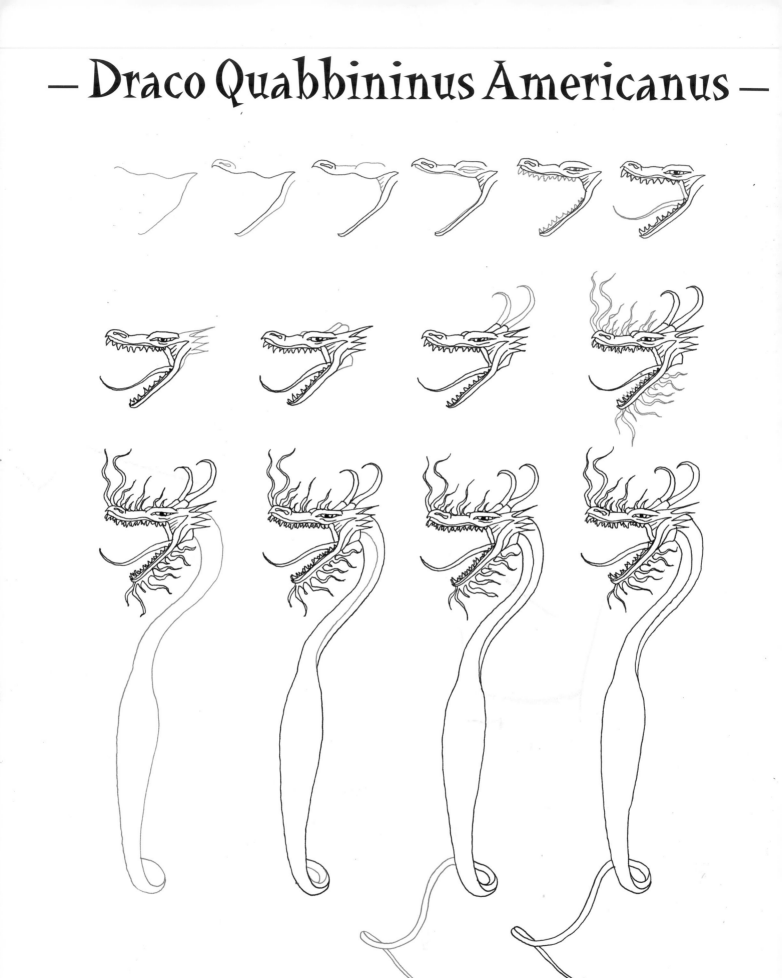

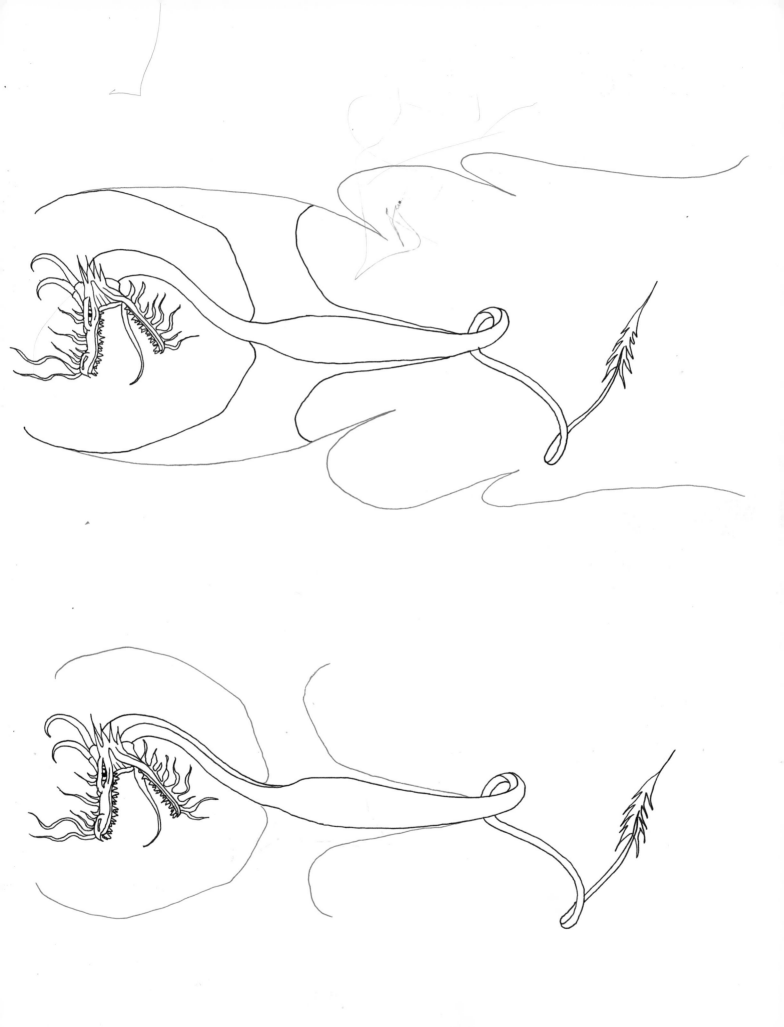

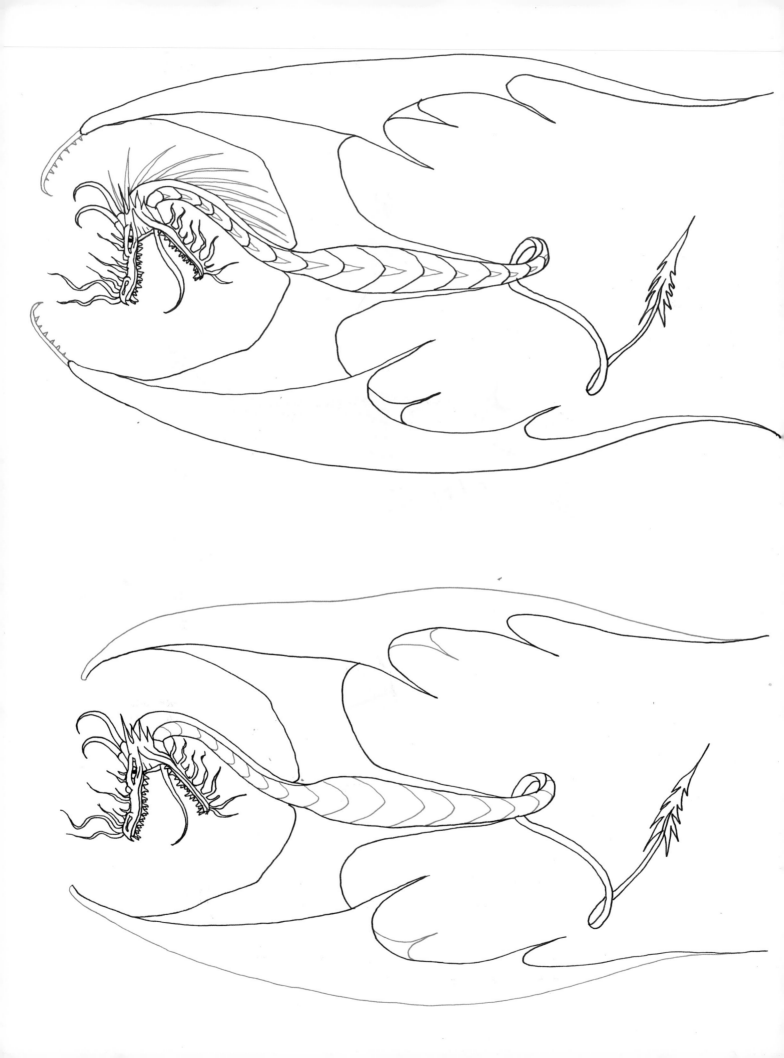

Are dragons real? Imagine and believe!

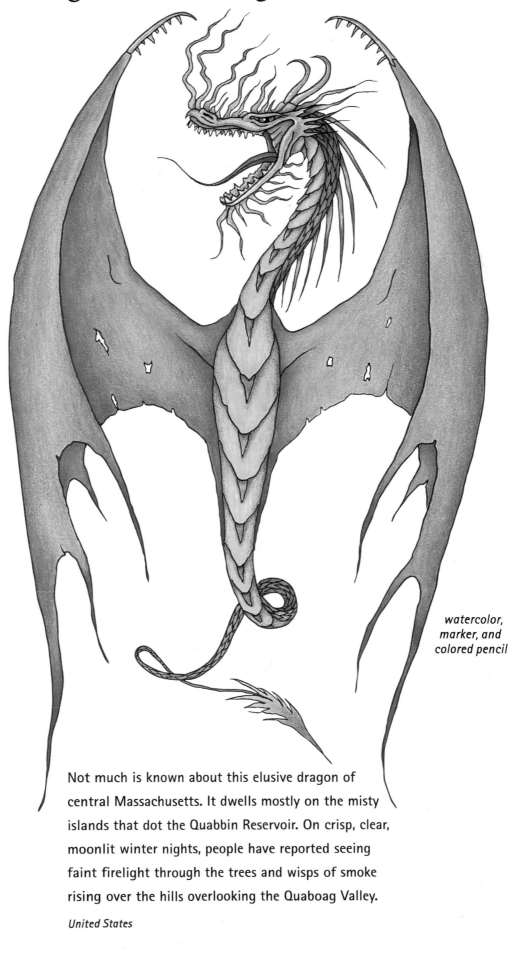

watercolor, marker, and colored pencil

Not much is known about this elusive dragon of central Massachusetts. It dwells mostly on the misty islands that dot the Quabbin Reservoir. On crisp, clear, moonlit winter nights, people have reported seeing faint firelight through the trees and wisps of smoke rising over the hills overlooking the Quaboag Valley.

United States

Resources

Books for Kids

Base, Graeme. *The Discovery of Dragons*. New York: Abrams, 1996.

Drake, Ernest. *Dr. Ernest Drake's Dragonology: The Complete Book of Dragons*. Cambridge, MA: Candlewick, 2003.

Hague, Michael. *The Book of Dragons*. New York: HarperCollins, 1995.

Books for Adults

Bulfinch, Thomas. *Bulfinch's Mythology*. Illustrated ed. New York: Gramercy Books, 2003.

Heuvelmans, Bernard. *On the Track of Unknown Animals*. 3rd ed. London: Kegan Paul International, 1995.

White, T. H., ed. and trans. *The Book of Beasts: Being a Translation from a Latin Bestiary of the Twelfth Century*. Mineola, NY: Dover, 1984.

Websites

Websites can change. Try running a search for *dragons* on your favorite search engine.

Dragons in Art and on the Web

http://www.isidore-of-seville.com/dragons/

Read about dragons in legend, literature, and film. Includes links to hundreds of other dragon websites.

Dragons in Children's Literature

http://www.ferrum.edu/thanlon/dragons/

Browse bibliographies of children's picture books, novels, anthologies, poems, and other resources.

Dragon Legends

http://www.mysteriousbritain.co.uk/legends/dragons.html

Journey to Britain through these dragon legends, including the tale of the Lambton Wyrm.

The Rainbow Serpent

http://www.nlc.org.au/html/abt_rainbow.html

Learn more about the rainbow serpent and Australian Aboriginal culture and history.

Pronunciation Guide

Aboriginal (a-buh-RIH-juh-nul)

Babylon (BA-buh-lawn)

Babylonian (BA-buh-LOH-nee-un)

cockatrice (KAW-kuh-trus)

Draco (DRAY-koh)

Fafnir (FAWF-nur)

makara (MAH-kah-rah, or mah-KAW-rah)

Mushussu (moo-SHOO-soo)

naga (NAW-guh)

ouroboros (or-ah-BOR-us)

Quabbin (KWAH-bin)

Quabbininus (kwah-BIN-nin-us)

Quaboag (KWAY-bog)

Siegfried (SIG-freed)

Sirrush (SEER-ush)

Wyrm (wurm)

wyvern (WIE-vurn)